FOCUS ON DISASTERS

Volcano

Fred Martin

Heinemann

First published in Great Britain by Heinemann Library
an imprint of Heinemann Publishers (Oxford) Ltd
Halley Court, Jordan Hill, Oxford OX2 8EJ

MADRID ATHENS PARIS
FLORENCE PRAGUE WARSAW
PORTSMOUTH NH CHICAGO SAO PAULO
SINGAPORE TOKYO MELBOURNE AUKLAND
IBADAN GABORONE JOHANNESBURG

© Heinemann Library 1995

Designed by Raynor Design

Produced by Mandarin Offset Ltd.
Printed and bound in China

99 98 97 96 95
10 9 8 7 6 5 4 3 2 1

ISBN 0 431 06837 2

British Library Cataloguing in Publication Data

Martin, Fred
Volcano - (Focus on Disasters Series)
I. Title II. Series
551.21

Acknowledgements
The Publishers would like to thank the following for permission to reproduce
photographs:
Ace Photo Agency: pp. 11, 30; Bruce Coleman Ltd: pp. 5, 8, 10, 12; Frank Spooner
Pictures: p. 27; G. Gerbasi Agenzia Contrasto/Katz Pictures Ltd: p. 29; GeoScience
Features: pp. 13, 23; Hutchison Library: pp. 32, 34; J. Allan Cash Photo Library: p. 40;
Michael Jay: pp. 16, 17, 38, 39, 41; Emile Luider/Rapho/Network: p. 36; Mats Wiße
Lund: pp. 20, 28; Planet Earth Pictures: p. 35; Popperfoto: p. 4; Robert Harding
Picture Library: pp.14, 37; Science Photo Library: pp. 7, 15, 19, 24, 26, 31, 33, 42,
43, 44, 45; Van Cappellen/REA/Katz Pictures Ltd: p. 25.

Cover photograph © Tony Stone Worldwide

Contents

The volcano story

THE power and unpredictable nature of volcanoes make them very dangerous and spectacular natural forces. A volcano is a hole in the planet's **crust** which ejects **molten rock**, **lava**, **ashes** and **gases**.

In September 1994, two volcanoes in Papua New Guinea exploded into life. Dense grey clouds of ash and pieces of red hot lava blasted into the air. The nearby landscape turned from green to grey as ash covered forests, fields, villages and towns.

The two volcanoes that erupted are Vulcan and Tarvurvur. They are on the island of New Britain in the south-west Pacific Ocean. In this part of the world at least one volcano **erupts** each year. Some of the most devastating **eruptions** on record have taken place in this area. Tambora and Krakatoa are two of the most powerful.

In 1815, the Tambora volcano suddenly erupted, blasting away most of its **cone**. About 10 000 people died in the blast and 80 000 more died as giant waves swept out from the volcano and drowned people on nearby islands. In 1883, the Krakatoa volcano erupted with the same kind of effect. Many volcanoes have erupted violently since Tambora and Krakatoa, but none matched their power or death toll.

Volcano study

Volcanoes are named after the Roman god Vulcan, who was the blacksmith who made weapons for the other gods. He was said to live on an island named Mount Vulcano near Sicily. The noise and fire from Mount Vulcano showed that Vulcan was at work in his forge.

Photo notes
- The eruptions of Vulcan and Tarvurvur began on 20 September 1994.
- They had not erupted for 57 years.
- People in Rabaul town had to escape.
- Within three days, Rabaul was under 91 cm of volcanic ash.
- One child was killed in a car accident and a man was killed by lightning from the volcanic cloud.

The ancient Romans knew about the effects of volcanic eruptions. In AD79, the Roman towns of Herculaneum and Pompeii were destroyed when Vesuvius erupted without warning. Both towns were buried under layers of ash until they were uncovered 1500 years later.

It is only in the last 250 years that scientists have begun to learn about why, how and when volcanoes erupt. In the 18th century, scientists and travellers went to Italy to study volcanoes that were known to erupt. Then it was realized that there used to be volcanoes in many other places. Volcanic rocks were found in the Massif Central in France. It was noticed that cone-shaped hills in the area were old volcanoes. Scientists also found old volcanic rocks in Scotland and in Germany.

In the last 30 years, **geologists** and other scientists have started to make sense of why and where volcanoes erupt. Knowing this will help save people's lives in the future. Many of the clues are deep under the Earth's hard outer layer and on the ocean beds. Better equipment and instruments now give more information about these places. There is better information about what materials come out of volcanoes and how volcanoes behave before they erupt.

DID YOU KNOW?

TV cameras were able to show the Vulcan and Tarvurvur volcanoes as soon as they erupted. In contrast, the first scientists did not get to the Tambora volcano until 32 years after it erupted in 1815.

Under the crust

To understand why volcanoes erupt, you have to know about what is inside the Earth. This is the source of the melted rock and gases that erupt from volcanoes. Rock that is so hot that it melts is called molten rock.

The layers inside

There are different layers inside the Earth. At the very centre, there is an **inner core** where temperatures are about 4300°C. Next there is an **outer core**, then a layer called the **lower mantle**. Even here,

temperatures are 3700°C. In the **upper mantle**, the temperatures are still high enough to melt rock. Molten rock in this layer is called **magma**.

Magma under pressure

Molten rock in the upper mantle is under great pressure. This means it stays solid until the pressure is released. It may help to think of the magma as a plastic which can only move, very slowly, when it is heated. Magma feeds volcanoes and flows through other cracks in the rocks above.

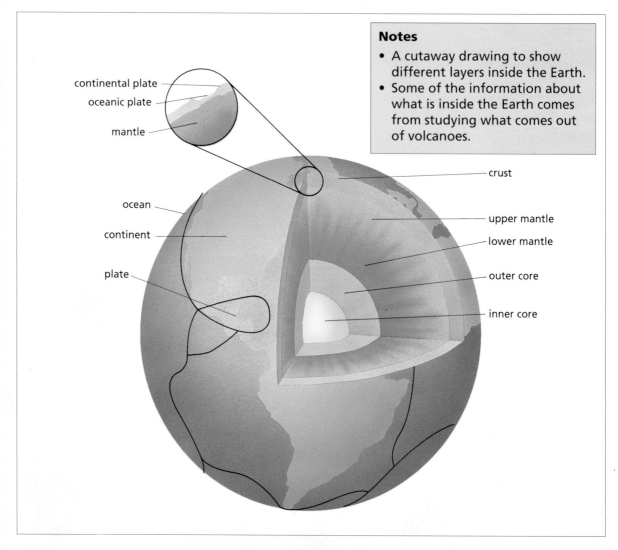

continental plate
oceanic plate
mantle

ocean
continent
plate

Notes
- A cutaway drawing to show different layers inside the Earth.
- Some of the information about what is inside the Earth comes from studying what comes out of volcanoes.

crust
upper mantle
lower mantle
outer core
inner core

The great pressure is released as it comes to the surface and escapes. This lowering of pressure allows the magma to become lava and flow more easily.

The thinnest layer

The thinnest of all the layers is the crust. This is the cooled, hard outer layer of the Earth. In places, the crust is only five kilometres thick. This is usually under the oceans. Under the continents, the crust may be about 50 km thick. Even here the crust is very thin when compared to the 6400 km radius of the Earth.

Even the crust is not all in one solid piece. It is split into large slabs called **plates**.

Photo notes
- Magma erupts from the Mauna Loa volcano in Hawaii.
- Molten rock at 1200°C comes out of a small vent on the volcano.
- The lava flows down the slopes until it cools down and hardens.

The plates are made of rock that is lighter and less **dense** than the material in the mantle. This means the plates are able to float on top of the mantle. Magma and other pieces of molten rock can force their way to the surface in places where the plates meet.

With such a thin layer of crust on top, it is not surprising that magma is able to force its way through from time to time. It is more surprising that it does not do so more often.

Inside a volcano

VOLCANOES are the mouth for the molten rock and gases from beneath the Earth's crust. A look inside a volcano shows how its different parts work.

The different parts

A volcano's cone is built up from layers of lava, ash and other materials that have erupted in the past. Each new eruption piles more material on top. Some cones are mostly made from layers of lava or **cinders**. Other have layers of different material such as ash, then lava, then more ash. These are called **composite cones**.

At the top of a volcano, there is a wide round opening called a **crater**. This is surrounded by a crater **rim**. In some craters, there are fiery pools of molten rock which bubble with escaping gases. In others, the lava has cooled down and become solid rock.

Inside the volcano, a narrow tube called a **pipe** leads down to the molten rock. The pipe has been opened up in the rocks by the heat and force of molten rock as it moves up. The top of the pipe is called the **vent**.

If lava in the crater has gone hard, it can form a **cap** over the top of the pipe. Sometimes a much larger **plug** blocks the pipe and the crater. Some of the most powerful eruptions have happened when a cap or plug has stopped magma rising up through the pipe. When this happens, pressure builds up until the blockage is suddenly blasted away.

A lake can form inside a crater when a volcano has not erupted for a long time. Sometimes the crater is filled in by loose rock that breaks off the rim. Snow and ice can also fill in the crater until the next eruption.

Photo notes
- The White Island volcano in New Zealand.
- Look at the wide round crater and the sharp edged crater rim.
- Part of the crater wall has been blown away by an explosion.
- More recent eruptions have started to build up a new cone inside the old crater.

The inner workings

At the bottom of the pipe, there is a giant pool of magma called a **magma chamber**. This acts as a reservoir that supplies the molten rock that comes out of the volcano.

The force of a volcanic eruption is caused by molten rock being forced up through the narrow pipe from the magma chamber.

Molten rock can also melt its way to the surface through other cracks and lines of weakness in the rocks. This can be through rocks near the volcano or even through the sides of the volcano. Molten rock in a crack that passes vertically through layers of rock is called a **dike**. When the molten rock flows between layers of rock, it is called a **sill**.

Smaller **conelets** can form on the slopes of a volcano. These are called **parasitic cones**. They show where a dike or sill has forced its way through the lava and ash that make up the volcano's sides.

Some volcanoes have a very long and active history. A cone can be built up then destroyed during a violent eruption. This does not mean the volcano has become extinct. A new, smaller cone can grow in its place. The Anak Krakatoa is a new volcano that has replaced the larger Krakatoa volcano that exploded and collapsed.

Notes
- A cross-section view into a typical volcano.
- The cone is built up from layers of different materials such as lava and ash.
- The volcano can have several smaller cones on its sides.

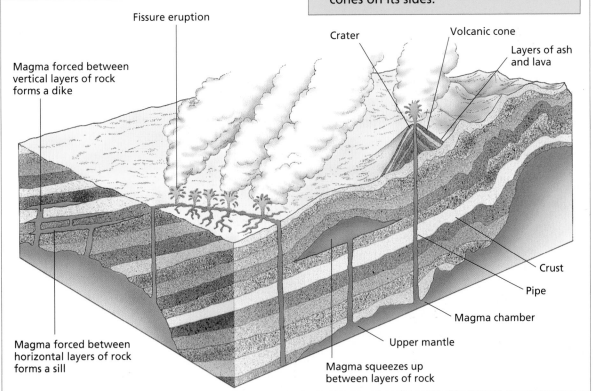

Fissure eruption

Crater

Volcanic cone

Layers of ash and lava

Magma forced between vertical layers of rock forms a dike

Magma forced between horizontal layers of rock forms a sill

Magma squeezes up between layers of rock

Upper mantle

Magma chamber

Pipe

Crust

Lava flows

MOLTEN rock pours out of a volcano and flows down the slopes as lava. At first, the temperature is about 1800°C, but as the lava flows down the slopes it cools. The flow slows down and stops as the lava cools and as it reaches more gentle slopes. A crust forms and the lava hardens. Most lavas form a type of rock called **basalt**.

Types of lava

Fast-flowing lava can race down slopes at 200 metres per second. When it cools, it looks like piles of rope. Lava that cools to this shape is called **pahoehoe**. The name comes from Hawaii where this type of lava is common. Lava can also creep at less than walking pace. When cool, this type of lava makes pasty blocks called **aa**.

The speed of the flow depends on the **minerals** and gases that are in the lava. There is often less **silica** in lavas that flow quickly than in those that flow more slowly. A high silica content makes lava more **viscous**. Silica is a common mineral in the Earth's crust.

Some lavas spread out and move forward along a wide front. Others flow in fast-moving, narrow streams. The outer layers of these streams cool first and form a hard skin which can be firm enough to walk on. Heat is kept inside the stream so the lava goes on flowing. When the lava drains away, the skin leaves a hollow tunnel called a **lava tube**.

Photo notes
- A flow of pahoehoe lava in the Galapagos islands.
- A skin of hard lava forms where the lava is cooled by the air.
- The lava cools down and forms thin folds that look like rope.

Floods of lava

Not all lava flows come out of the vent of a volcano. They also come from long cracks called **fissures**. These fissures can be 100 kilometres long and 30 metres wide. A flood of lava flows out and buries everything in its path. The largest of these lava flows are called **flood basalts**. In some places flood basalt spills out on to the landscape to form a **plateau**. There is evidence that this happened six million years ago in what is now the Columbia River plateau in the USA. Other flood basalts are found in Northern Ireland and in the Deccan uplands of India. Flood basalts can be hundreds of metres thick and build up to even greater depths if they flow into an area of lowland.

Some of nature's most unusual landscapes are caused by these flood basalts. As the lava cools, it starts to shrink. The effect looks similar to soil that has started to dry out. The rock cracks into regular six-sided shapes. These can be seen as tall hexagonal pillars. The pillars stretch from the top to the bottom of the basalt.

Fortunately, unlike volcanic eruptions, flood basalts do not occur very often. The largest were formed many millions of years ago. There have been none within recorded historic time. The fact that they have happened in the past almost certainly means that they could happen again.

DID YOU KNOW?

The Giant's Causeway in Northern Ireland, Fingal's Cave in Scotland and the Devil's Postpile in California are three places where the regular hexagons can be seen. They make interesting places for tourists to visit. Their unusual shapes make them look unnatural so stories have been told about them. The Giant's Causeway is said to be part of a giant's stepping stones from Ireland to Scotland.

Volcano shapes

THERE are about 600 volcanoes on Earth that are still likely to erupt. These are called **active volcanoes**. There is usually a large eruption from at least one active volcano every year.

Some volcanoes have not erupted for thousands of years but they may erupt again in the future. These are **dormant volcanoes**. Dormant means 'sleeping'.

There are also **extinct volcanoes** that will never erupt again. There may be little left of these after rain, frost, ice and wind have worn them down.

Volcanic cones

Most volcanoes can be recognized by their cone shape. There are no other natural shapes in the landscape that look like them. Some rise from a flat surrounding landscape or from the sea bed. Others are parts of mountain ranges. Some of the Earth's tallest mountains are volcanoes. In South America, Japan and Indonesia, some volcanic cones rise to over 6000 m.

The steepness of the cone depends on what has come out of the volcano. Sticky, slow lava or large pieces of rock do not travel far, so they pile up as steep slopes. Runny, fast-flowing lava travels a long way and makes shallow slopes. Other materials from volcanoes, such as cinders, fall to the ground and come to rest at a different angle. Many cones are built up from layers of different materials. This means that there is a great variety in the shapes and sizes of volcanoes.

In Hawaii volcanoes have shallow slopes. Mauna Loa is one of the largest. It is built up from the bed of the Pacific Ocean so its base is about 100 km wide.

Photo notes
- The cone of the Semeru volcano in Indonesia is in the background.
- In the foreground, steep slopes and sharp ridges show the remains of old craters.

Photo notes
- Part of the Mauna Loa active volcano in Hawaii.
- The low slope angle on a shield volcano shows that the lava is very runny.
- Notice the dark-coloured recent lava flow.

Mauna Loa is an example of a **shield volcano**. It looks like a shield lying on its back. Shield volcanoes are this shape because the lava that flows from them is very runny and fast-flowing. It can flow a long way at a very low angle. Each flow is covered by lava from the next eruption.

How volcanoes grow

The height and shape of the cone of a volcano depend on several things. If the volcano is still active, each new eruption builds it higher. A new volcano can grow from nothing to several hundred metres high within a few months. The volcanic island of Surtsey near Iceland did this in 1963. In a few months, it grew from the ocean bed to form an island 2.5 square kilometres in area and several hundred metres high. A smaller cone then began to grow beside the main cone but this was washed away by the sea. The Surtsey volcano itself may erupt again and become even larger. But, in the end, it too will be washed away by the sea.

Volcanoes can also change shape. This can happen if a violent eruption blows away a large part of the cone. The 1980 eruption of Mount St Helens in north-west USA blew away the top and left a half open crater where the cone had been.

DID YOU KNOW?

The Hawaiian islands are all volcanoes that have grown up from the bed of the Pacific Ocean. The total height of Mauna Loa is about 10 000 metres but only the top 4205 metres are above sea level. This is higher than Mount Everest which is about 1500 metres lower. Many of the volcanoes in Hawaii are still active, but their eruptions are not usually violent.

Types of eruption

VOLCANOES erupt in many different ways. Even the same volcano can erupt in different ways at different times. At one extreme, there are violent explosions that blast material high into the atmosphere and out into the surrounding landscape. There are also more gentle eruptions where puffs of ash and gases are released without causing much damage.

The type of eruption depends mostly on the materials inside the volcano's magma chamber. The shape of the volcano and how the cone behaves during the eruption affect the eruption itself.

What comes out

The force of an eruption partly depends on what is being erupted. Magma that is low in silica and high in gases tends to erupt gently. Runny lava flows out of the crater or out through side conelets. These are called **effusive eruptions**. Eruptions from the wide craters of the volcanoes in Hawaii are often like this. In smaller eruptions, the lava does not even flow out of the crater.

There is a more violent eruption when water mixes with the molten rock. The water instantly turns to steam and the effect is like an exploding steam boiler. This is called a **steam eruption**. Water can come in contact with magma in two ways.

Photo notes
- Lava in a crater on Kilauea in Hawaii.
- The lava is runny so that it flows easily down the slopes before it cools down and goes hard.
- This is an example of an effusive eruption.

It can meet with water that is in the underground rocks. Sea water rushing into a collapsing crater can have the same effect. This is what happened during the giant eruption at Krakatoa in 1883.

Different types of gas are also ejected. These include carbon dioxide, nitrogen and sulphur dioxide. The amount of gas affects the force of the eruption.

Flying debris

Pieces of all sizes are blasted out of a volcano during an eruption. The largest pieces spin around and change their shape to become streamlined. These are called **volcanic bombs**. Volcanic bombs can weigh up to 100 tonnes.

More powerful eruptions blast the molten rock into even smaller pieces. The result is a giant cloud of dust and ash. When Vesuvius erupted in AD79, most of the deaths in the Roman town of Pompeii were caused by a cloud of dust, ash and gas. The people choked to death as they tried to escape. This is called a **Plinian explosion**, after a Roman writer named Pliny who died during the eruption.

Some eruptions throw out larger pieces of **pumice** and cinders. Pumice has tiny holes in it where there were gas bubbles. There are so many holes in pumice that it can float on water. The gas holes in cinders are larger. The mixture of ash and larger solid pieces is called **tuff**. Thick layers of tuff can pile up near a volcano.

One of the most dangerous types of volcanic eruption is when ash, cinders and pumice are blasted out in a burning cloud. The material travels quickly over a long distance. The cloud is called a *nuée ardente* which means 'a glowing cloud' in French.

Photo notes
- An eruption from Mount St Helens in Washington state, USA.
- This eruption came two months after the larger eruption which blew away part of the volcano on the side away from the photograph.
- The cloud of debris is made of grey ash, and other tiny pieces of rock and gases.
- This is an example of a Plinian eruption.

In 1902, the town of St Pierre on the West Indian island of Martinique was hit by a *nuée ardente* from the nearby Mount Pelée volcano. All but two of the town's 30 000 people were killed.

One type of eruption that can catch people unexpectedly is when the side of a crater is blown out, sending all the force sideways instead of up. This happened in the Mount St Helens eruption of 1980. People 25 kilometres away thought they were safe, but they were wrong. Many died because they were on the side that blew out.

DID YOU KNOW?

Scientists think that gas from volcanic eruptions over millions of years helped to form the Earth's early atmosphere.

Rocks from volcanoes

ALL rocks can be put into one of three groups. **Sedimentary rocks** are made from pieces of plants or animals and from the broken pieces of other rocks. **Metamorphic rocks** have been heated and compressed so much that they have changed from their original type of rock. The third group are called **igneous rocks**. *Ignis* is the Latin word for fire. These rocks have come from under the Earth's surface, sometimes through a volcano.

Extrusive rocks

Basalt that flows from a volcano as lava is a type of igneous rock. Igneous rocks that come to the surface and then cool down are called **extrusive rocks**. To extrude means 'to push through and to come out'.

Basalt is a heavy, dark coloured rock. Like other rocks, basalt is made of several minerals that have been joined by great heat and pressure. A mineral is a pure substance that has its own features and chemical properties. Individual minerals in basalt can be seen as very small **crystals**.

Crystals grow and take their shape as the minerals cool down. Basalt cools quickly because it comes out into the air or meets cold rock near the surface. This is why the crystals in basalt are so small. They have not had time to grow.

Photo notes
- The top of basalt columns in the Devil's Postpile, California.
- About a million years ago, lava flowed into the area and cooled down slowly.
- The air cooled the top layer and cold rock underneath cooled the bottom.
- The tops of the columns in this photo have been polished by glaciers that moved over them.

Some volcanic rocks such as **obsidian** look like black shiny glass. Their minerals have been baked then cooled very quickly.

Rocks that intrude

Not all igneous rocks cool down quickly at or near the surface. Instead, some of them cool down deep underground. **Granite** is this type. A mass of magma rises up into the crust but does not break through to the surface. Instead, it cools slowly and becomes solid rock. Rocks formed in this way are called **intrusive rocks**. They are like an intruder because they have moved through the rock above them.

Granite is an easy rock to identify though it can have many different colours. Like basalt, it is hard and very heavy, but it looks different because it is much easier to see the mineral crystals.

There are three main minerals in granite. There are large crystals of milky coloured **quartz** and chunks of **feldspar** that can be pink, green or other colours. There are also small flakes of a shiny mineral called **mica**. The crystals are so large in granite because the rock has cooled down underground very slowly. They have had plenty of time to grow.

Granite and other intrusive rocks can often be seen on the Earth's surface.

DID YOU KNOW?

There are no active volcanoes in Britain but there are many places where there are different types of igneous rocks. Some are basalts that are only 30 million years old. There are also areas of granite that are nearly 3000 million years old.

This happens when the layers of rock above them are worn away over millions of years. Granite that forms the plateau of Dartmoor in England cooled down about 200 million years ago. Since then, thousands of metres of softer sedimentary rocks above the granite have been stripped away, leaving the granite exposed. Granite often forms high land because it is harder than the rocks around it. They have worn down faster, leaving the granite high up.

Photo notes
- A granite tor on Dartmoor.
- As the softer rocks above are worn away, the granite is able to expand and large cracks form in it.
- Rain and frost get into the cracks and make them deeper and wider.

Where are volcanoes?

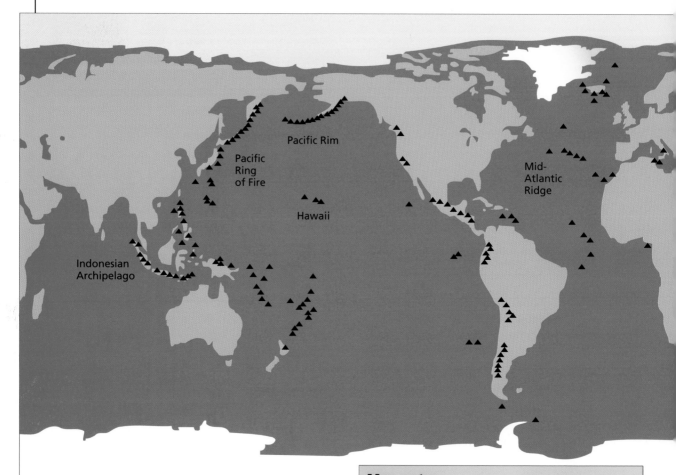

Pacific Rim

Pacific Ring of Fire

Mid-Atlantic Ridge

Hawaii

Indonesian Archipelago

Map notes
- Volcanoes are mainly in lines that run along the edges of continents and through the middle of oceans.
- There is a separate group of volcanoes in the middle of the Pacific Ocean.

LOOK at a world map that shows where the active volcanoes are. You need to know where they are to understand why they erupt only in some places.

Lines of volcanoes

Volcanoes are not spread everywhere over the Earth. There are some definite patterns to where they exist.

It is easy to see that volcanoes are in lines that run for thousands of kilometres. Some of the lines are near where a continent meets an ocean. There are volcanoes near to where the South American continent meets the Pacific

Ocean. There are also volcanoes where the Pacific Ocean meets the islands and coastline of Asia.

There are lines of volcanoes down the middle of some oceans. There are volcanoes in Iceland halfway across the Atlantic Ocean. The line continues through the Atlantic Ocean as small volcanic islands. Ascension Island is one of these. Others are below the surface so they cannot be seen.

Photo notes

- A line of seven volcanoes in Java where the Pacific Ocean meets Asia.
- Small patches of white cloud are around each volcanic cone.
- These volcanoes are still active and some could be a serious hazard to people who live nearby.
- An eruption and giant waves could cause many deaths.

There is one unusual group of volcanoes in the Hawaiian Islands in the middle of the Pacific Ocean. These do not seem to be part of a longer line of volcanoes.

Making sense

The lines of volcanoes go in a patchwork of giant irregular circles. This makes the map like a giant jig-saw puzzle. There are so many volcanoes around the Pacific Ocean that it is often called the **Pacific Ring of Fire**.

In October 1994, one of the 'Ring of Fire' volcanoes erupted, sending clouds of volcanic dust 20 000 metres high into the atmosphere. This came from the Klyuchevskay volcano on the Russian Kamchatka peninsula. Aircraft were warned not to go near in case engines became clogged with the dust.

There are groups of volcanoes in some places. This happens in places like Iceland, Japan and the islands of Indonesia. Some of these are called **island arcs**.

You also need to see where there are no volcanoes. Places away from the edges of the continents seem to be safe from them and there are vast areas of ocean where there are no volcanoes.

The places where volcanoes are found must have something in common. Remember that the Earth's crust is divided into large plates. The lines where plates meet are in the same place as the lines of volcanoes. Something must be happening along the edges of these plates to cause the volcanoes. There must be some kind of split in the crust which allows molten rock from inside the Earth to escape to the surface. The split must be moving so this can happen.

DID YOU KNOW? ?

Six out of every ten volcanoes in the world are around the Pacific Ocean in the Pacific Ring of Fire.

Volcanoes and plates

IT has been known for a long time that an undersea ridge runs down the middle of the Atlantic Ocean. There is also a broken line of volcanoes along this line. Some appear as islands though most do not appear above the surface. Since the 1960s, it has been known that this is a line between two of the Earth's plates. To the east is the Eurasian plate. To the west is the North American plate.

Ocean ridges and volcanoes

About 100 million years ago, the North American **land mass** was joined to the Eurasian land mass. They were both on one very large continental plate. Then the plates began to split apart. The plates moved very slowly and over a very long time. Their movement opened up the Atlantic Ocean. The plates are still pulling apart, making Europe and North America further from each other each year.

As the plates pull apart, a large crack is made in the Earth's thin crust. This crack is called a **rift**. Magma is able to rise up through the rift. This has built up volcanic cones in some places.

The magma oozes out on the ocean bed on both sides of the rift. It rolls out and then quickly cools. Pressure from the water above forces the magma to form into rounded shapes. This is called **pillow lava** because it looks like piles of pillows when it cools down. Slowly, the lava spreads over the ocean bed to form new areas of crust.

Why plates move

Something must be causing the Earth's plates to move. One idea is that magma beneath the crust moves like currents in hot air or a liquid that is being heated. These are called **convection currents**. The currents rise from inside the mantle until they reach the crust.

Photo notes
- A fissure eruption near Heimaey in Iceland.
- Lava shoots into the air as the plates pull apart.
- Lava flows out and cools on the ground.

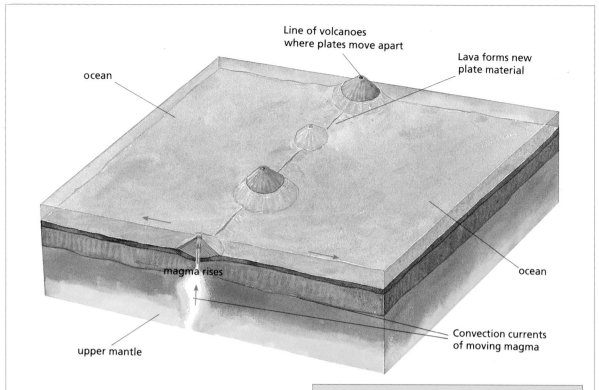

Line of volcanoes where plates move apart

Lava forms new plate material

ocean

ocean

magma rises

upper mantle

Convection currents of moving magma

Then they divide and flow away from each other beneath the crust. As they move, they drag the plates along with them. This is part of a **theory** called **plate tectonics**. It helps explain why and where some volcanoes erupt. It also helps explain why some earthquakes happen in the same areas. It is believed that where the edges of plates drag against each other, they sometimes get locked together. Tremendous strain builds up until eventually the plates suddenly unjam themselves. This shakes the ground violently as the plates move past each other.

The group of volcanoes in the middle of the Pacific Ocean may be caused in a different way. They are not near any rift in a plate. Instead, several rising convection currents may be coming up beneath the crust in this area. This forms a **hot spot** in the crust. Volcanoes form where some of the magma forces its way through the layers of rock above. The volcanoes in Hawaii are probably caused in this way.

Notes
- The Earth's hard outer crust is divided into separate slabs called plates.
- They are separated by lines of weakness called faults or rifts.
- Plate movements help explain why there are volcanoes in some places.

In the past, scientists have had many theories that have proved to be wrong. It is very hard to collect the evidence needed to prove the plate tectonics theory. People cannot go under the Earth's crust to see convection currents. Even instruments cannot be sent that deep and survive the great heat and pressure. As more information becomes available, theories change and new ones replace them.

DID YOU KNOW?

Scientists can measure how fast the plates are moving by using **satellite images**. Plates move between 5 and 10 cm in a year. Even this small distance can be recorded accurately from space.

Plates that collide

THE theory of plate tectonics describes how rising convection currents reach the crust then pull the plates along with their movement. There are places where plates are moving towards each other. These are the places where the most violent eruptions happen.

Melting plates

One place where two plates are colliding is along the west coast of South America. As the South American plate moves west, it collides with the smaller Nazca plate that is moving east. Something has to give way when two plates meet.

As the convection current goes back into the upper mantle, it pulls the smaller Nazca plate down with it. This forms an **ocean trench** which is much deeper than the rest of the ocean bed.

As the Nazca plate is dragged down further, it slides under the larger South American plate. This area is called the **subduction zone**. By about twenty kilometres down, the temperature and pressure are enough to make the plate rock break up and become molten.

As the smaller Nazca plate sinks into the mantle, the advancing edge of the South American plate is buckled upwards. Layers of sedimentary rocks are folded up to form the Andes mountain chain.

Notes
- Plates move towards each other in some parts of the Earth.
- Plate rock melts as it slides under another plate.
- The molten rock rises back to the surface to form volcanoes.

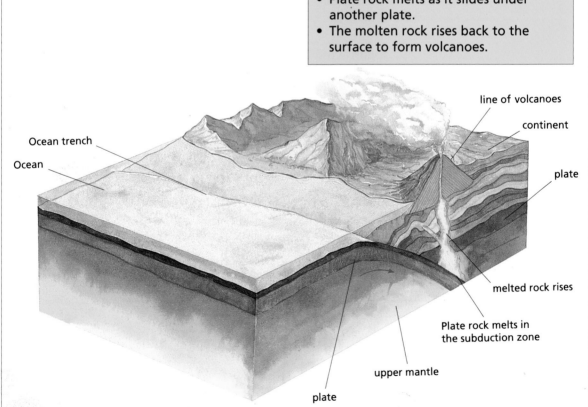

Ocean trench

Ocean

line of volcanoes

continent

plate

melted rock rises

Plate rock melts in the subduction zone

upper mantle

plate

Volcanoes break out

Rock from the end of the melting plate is not as dense as the material in the mantle around it. Water and gases have also been dragged down with it. The melted rock starts to move back up towards the Earth's surface, melting and forcing its way up through lines of weakness in the layers of rock above. This is easier because rocks at the edge of the plate above crack and bend by the force of the collision.

The molten rock moves up and collects in a magma chamber before passing through either a single pipe or long fissures. The force of the eruption that follows is caused by the sudden release of material that has been under such great pressure.

There have been several recent examples of eruptions above subduction zones. In 1985, the Nevado del Ruiz volcano in Colombia erupted, killing 25 000 people in a flood and mudslide. In 1991, the Galeras volcano in Colombia erupted, forcing people to move out of the area. In 1993, Galeras erupted again killing a British geologist who was studying it.

DID YOU KNOW?

The deepest part of all of the oceans is the Marianas trench near the Philippines. This trench is 11.3 km deep. The trench is where the Pacific plate starts to dip underneath the Indo-Australian plate.

On the opposite side of the Pacific Ocean, volcanoes were also becoming more active. The Pinatubo volcano in the Philippines erupted violently in 1991. Mount Unzen in Japan erupted in the same year. In 1993, the Mayon volcano in the Philippines erupted 26 times on one day.

Eruptions in these places will go on for as long as the plates continue to collide there, so there is a supply of molten rock to feed the volcanoes. Most of the present plates will still be moving for millions of years.

Photo notes
- The Fuego volcano in Guatemala is 3600 metres high and is still active.
- This is one of about 50 volcanoes in Central America.
- These volcanoes are all above a subduction zone where plate material is always melting and moving to the surface.

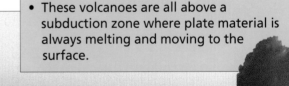

Pinatubo erupts

MOUNT Pinatubo in the Philippines was a dormant volcano until June 1991. It had been dormant for 600 years so it was not thought of as dangerous. Farmers had built villages near it to use the rich volcanic soil. The US Air Force had built an airfield only sixteen kilometres away and there was also a large US naval base nearby. By 9 June 1991, everything was set for the disaster that was soon to follow.

The sky turns grey

On 10 June, a ten-kilometre stream of mud and lava flowed down the volcano's slopes. It raced at 80 kilometres per hour, wrecking homes and crops in its way. Fifteen thousand people had to flee immediately from the area. There were four minor eruptions that may have been a sign that worse was to come. Three days later, there were several violent eruptions over a period of twenty hours. Ash was thrown twenty kilometres high into the air.

The danger zone was extended to 30 kilometres, then a few days later to 40 kilometres. By then, a fissure three kilometres long had opened up on the side of the volcano.

People feared a violent blast from the side of the volcano, just like the eruption at Mount St Helens in 1980. Fortunately this kind of eruption did not happen. The vast amounts of ash and the **mudflows** were to cause the greatest problems.

Things got worse while the eruptions were still taking place. An earthquake rocked the area, bringing its own problems.

Then a **typhoon** roared in, blowing the ash in all directions. Heavy rain loosened ash and soil, and caused even more mudslides.

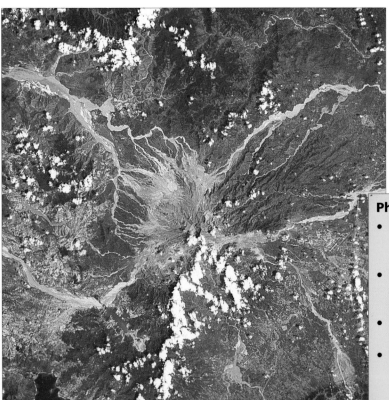

Photo notes
- The crater of Mount Pinatubo is in the centre of the photograph.
- Mud and ash from the 1991 eruption fill the valleys down the slopes of the volcano.
- Farmland and villages are around the base of the volcano.
- The runways of the US Air Force base can be seen to the right.

Photo notes
- Thick ash from the Mount Pinatubo eruption blots out the sun, even during daytime, as people try to flee.
- Everything is covered with the fine ash.

Counting the cost

The volcano continued to erupt for the next three months, though not with the same force as before. The worst of the damage had already been done.

The final death toll was about 350. Some people were killed in the mudflows that raced down the volcano's slopes and into the river valleys. Even more were killed in their homes and other buildings. The weight of ash was too much for many of the farmhouses, which had been built with wooden posts supporting roofs made from rice straw. Some people were killed when the roof of a school collapsed. In the panic to get away from the volcano, some people died in car accidents.

Almost 200 000 people are said to have been affected. Many were made homeless. Others lost their crops when ash and mudflows covered their fields. In Manila, the capital city, people had to dig the ash away from their homes. Breathing the air caused problems for people who had asthma and other breathing difficulties.

The Mount Pinatubo eruption was caused because the small Philippine plate is slowly moving west and sliding under the larger Indo-Australian plate. Plate rock melts and makes its way to the surface through Mount Pinatubo and other volcanoes in the area. This means that there is every chance that Mount Pinatubo will erupt again. It might be dormant for another 600 years or it may erupt much sooner. Nobody knows when or what will happen. Until then, living anywhere near Mount Pinatubo is going to be a risk.

DID YOU KNOW? **?**

After the eruption, an officer from the US Subic Bay naval base near Mount Pinatubo was heard to say, 'Our base is grey, the same colour as our ships.'

Predicting an eruption

THE best way to avoid death and damage from a volcanic eruption is to be able to give an accurate **prediction** of when one will happen. People also need to know how violent the eruption will be and what will come out of the volcano. A few weeks' or even a few days' warning is needed so that people can get away and emergency services can be made ready.

Study the past

Geologists have found some ways to make predictions about how a volcano might behave. Old eruptions are studied by looking at layers of rock on the slopes and in the nearby landscape. Satellite images are used to map where old lava flows have gone. Layers of lava, ash and other volcanic materials are dated to build up a picture of when the volcano has erupted and what has come out of it. Information from paintings, old newspapers and other written records can also be used.

When a volcano starts to erupt, geologists rush to the area to measure what is happening. Learning about the behaviour of one volcano can help to understand how others might behave. Every detail is important. The temperature of the lava, the minerals in it and the types of gas can all give clues about what is happening.

This information helps to find out which volcanoes are most likely to erupt and how dangerous the eruption is likely to be.

Photo notes
- Two geologists study a lava flow on Mauna Loa in Hawaii.
- Information about what minerals are in the lava and how hot it is helps to make predictions about how the volcano might behave in the future.
- Protective clothes need to be worn for this work.

Measuring volcanoes

Geologists use **observatories** on some volcanoes to watch and measure what is happening inside. **Tiltmeters** measure if the slopes are changing their shape and angle. **Lasers** can do this, but they are expensive. If magma is slowly rising into the volcano, the slopes may start to bulge. This happened in 1980 before the Mount St Helens eruption, but it was not possible to predict enough about the eruption.

Rising magma may give off unusual gases. Measurements can be taken to check for any changes. Gases were measured before the Mount St Helens eruption but no changes were found.

Seismometers can detect small movements in the ground, which people cannot feel. Ground movements can be caused by normal earthquakes or by magma forcing its way up under the volcano. Some animals can feel these movements and start to behave differently.

An earthquake can be the trigger that cracks the ground and releases pressure inside the volcano. Earthquakes were recorded for months before the Mount St Helens eruption. In the end a massive earthquake shook the volcano with no warning. It caused a **landslide** on one side of the volcano and within seconds there was a violent explosion as the molten rock was exposed. The blast of gas, rock and ash flattened trees up to 26 km away. Sixty people died. One was a geologist who had been measuring the volcano. Trying to predict an eruption is a valuable but very dangerous job. Even if the date of an eruption is predicted, people need to know how far away to go to be safe.

Damage control

NOBODY has found a way to stop a volcano erupting. The power that is released is far too great to control. There does not seem to be anything anyone can do except to get as far away, as quickly as possible.

Good thinking

In 1973, the Helgafell volcano erupted behind the town of Heimaey in Iceland. All 5000 people were able to get away safely. Volcanoes are nothing new to the people of Iceland. There are many active volcanoes both on the mainland and on the islands around it. That is why the people of Heimaey had already planned that boats and aeroplanes would be ready to evacuate them.

Some people stayed behind to fight the volcano. Someone had an idea that if the lava could be cooled, it would slow down and might even stop. Hoses were brought to within a few metres of the lava and millions of litres of seawater were sprayed on it. It is hard to tell if this worked, but the lava did slow down and most of the town was saved.

This way of stopping lava may have some chance of working in other places. The problems are that not all lava flows as slowly as this and many places do not have either the water or the equipment to make use of it.

Fighting back

Mount Etna in Sicily is an active volcano with a long history of regular eruptions. On many occasions in the past, lava has flowed down the slopes and destroyed homes and farmland.

People who live near Etna have found some ways to reduce the damage. They divert the lava to where it will do least damage. They do this by digging or using dynamite to blast out a new route for the lava to follow. The sides of a lava flow usually harden first.

Photo notes
- Water pipes are being brought up to the lava which is flowing from the Helgafell eruption at Heimaey.
- Some houses have already been set on fire and have been crushed by the lava.
- Hoses sprayed cold sea water onto the lava to make it cool and form a hard skin.

Photo notes
- In 1992, a lava flow from Mount Etna in Sicily looked as if it would destroy people's homes.
- Bulldozers and mechanical shovels were used to build a dam to stop the lava.

By breaking through the sides, the lava's route can be diverted. Another method is to block the lava's route by pushing up high walls of rock and earth using bulldozers. Helicopters are used to drop large blocks of rock to make a dam against the lava. This has been successful and, for the people of Sicily, it seems to be the only way to fight their local volcano.

Some buildings and even complete towns are never rebuilt after a volcanic eruption. Sometimes the whole landscape is changed and it is impossible to go back. Roman Pompeii is one town that was never rebuilt. After the eruption in AD79, it lay under the ash and lava from Vesuvius for 1500 years.

The story is very different in other places. The people of Heimaey tried to save their houses by sweeping ash off their roofs as it fell. As soon as the eruption had stopped, they moved back and dug out as much of the town as they could.

When people rebuild in the same place, perhaps they think the volcano will not erupt again for some time. Volcanoes may lie dormant for hundreds of years. People may think they have survived one eruption, so they can survive another. They may not have anywhere else to go. People who live near volcanoes get to know them and learn to live with the risks.

DID YOU KNOW?

The first recorded attempt to divert a flow of lava was in 1669. Lava was flowing from Mount Etna towards the town of Catania. The hard side skin of the lava was broken so that the lava could flow out and down a different route, but the lava flowed towards a nearby village instead. The villagers forced the townspeople to stop their work. In the end, the lava flowed into the town and destroyed a large part of it.

Hot water

A free supply of hot water is one of the few advantages of living near a volcano. Underground water is naturally heated by the hot volcanic rocks. Water heated in the way is called **hydrothermal**.

Geysers and hot springs

Hot water **geysers** are one of the unusual features of volcanic areas. A fountain of steam and hot water shoots up from under the ground. Some do this regularly. In Yellowstone National Park in the USA, Old Faithful erupts every 70 minutes or so.

The water begins as rainwater that has trickled deep into the rocks below. It collects in layers of **porous** rock where there are tiny spaces between the grains.

The hot volcanic rocks heat up the water to well above normal boiling point. There is great pressure underground so the water can stay **superheated** without changing to steam. The geyser erupts when superheated water rises up and meets the colder water trickling down from above. When enough new cold water has collected and been heated, the same thing happens again.

Bursts of steam and gases also come out through **fumaroles**, where superheated water comes up to the surface from deep reservoirs of porous rock. Some hot water comes out as **springs** and may flow as rivers, bringing minerals to the surface that can stain the rocks bright colours such as red and yellow.

In places, the ground bubbles, making **mudpots** and larger **mud volcanoes**. These form when boiling water mixes with fine soil and builds up a small mound of erupting mud.

Photo notes
- A geyser erupting in New Zealand at Whakarewarewa.
- The powerful jet of superheated water boils and turns to steam when the pressure on it is released.
- There will be another eruption when more water trickles down to be heated by the hot volcanic rock.

Using the water

Some people believe that bathing in hot water heated by volcanic rocks is good for their health. The town of Beppu on Kyushu island in Japan attracts more than ten million visitors every year to its hot water baths. People who suffer from arthritis and rheumatism are helped by the soothing waters. Minerals in the water may also help cure some skin diseases.

There is a vast amount of heat under the Earth's crust. This heat can be a useful source of energy to generate electricity. One way to get this energy is to make use of hot underground water.

Power stations have been built which use the force of steam to turn **turbines**. The turbines are linked to generators to produce electricity. All that is needed is a supply of underground hot water. There is no air pollution like that from burning coal or oil. The energy does not depend on the weather, unlike energy from the wind or the sun.

Another advantage is that unlike nuclear power, there are no safety problems.

Energy produced in this way is called **geothermal energy**. In the future, water may be pumped into the ground in places where there are hot rocks within a few kilometres of the surface. This could give an endless supply of electricity.

DID YOU KNOW?

The Vikings in Iceland used hot water from springs 1000 years ago. Today, people in the city of Reykjavik use the hot water as central heating for their homes. There is no pollution from the hot water so this helps make Reykjavik one of the world's cleanest cities.

Volcanic soils

Photo notes
- Farmland in Japan at the foot of a volcano.
- Lava and ash have broken down to become fertile soil.
- People think about the risk of an eruption but also want to use the best farmland.

IT may seem odd that anyone wants to live near a volcano but there is at least one very good reason why many people do. The land around volcanoes and even on their slopes is often used for farming because the soil is very **fertile**.

Mineral rich

The ancient Romans grew crops on the slopes of Vesuvius before their cities at Pompeii and Herculaneum were destroyed. Long after the eruption, farmers returned to the area and grew crops on the ash that was covering the cities. Crops are grown on the slopes of Mount Etna in spite of the danger from regular lava flows. The steep slopes of volcanoes in Japan and Indonesia are cut into terraces so the land can be farmed.

The reason for this is that volcanic rocks are rich in minerals and therefore they are very fertile. As the rock breaks down, minerals that are needed by crops are left in the soil that is formed.

After a volcanic eruption, the lava, ash and other materials are dumped on the surrounding landscape. This makes the area look bare and useless. Trees and other vegetation can be blasted away. The land still steams as the hot lava cools down.

New growth

Nature has a way of making even this kind of landscape turn green again. The rain and wind soon start to work on the new rock. Even as the lava is cooling, the rain and wind begin to break it down again. Heat from the day's sun, then cooling at night, make the rock expand and contract. This makes it weaker until pieces begin to flake off or shatter. The ways the weather breaks up rock are called **weathering**.

Some plants manage to survive an eruption and break through the ash. Once they are growing again, their seeds quickly spread to start new plants. Seeds are also carried by the wind, by birds and by other animals.

A new volcanic island was formed near Iceland in 1963. Within months, vegetation was starting to grow on the island. Scientists found that birds were bringing some of the new seeds. Other types of vegetation and animals arrived on rafts of floating driftwood. Mosses and lichens took root on the lava. Their roots and acids in the vegetation along with weathering helped break down the rock.

Soil is formed as pieces of broken rock are mixed with the rotting vegetation. As the soil becomes deeper and more fertile, more plants and animals move to the area.

This is what has been happening to the area around the Mount St Helens volcano. The eruption in 1980 blasted away the forests and covered the area with ash. Yet within a few months, new vegetation was starting to break through. Within a hundred years, the landscape could be covered in trees again. This is a very short time in nature.

Photo notes
- Thistles start to break through the ash near the Mount St Helens volcano.
- Rain has formed small streams that wash away the ash and expose the soil below.
- Seeds from the thistles will spread and more will grow.
- Other types of vegetation will also start to appear, a new soil will form and the natural wildlife and vegetation will come back.

Wealth from volcanoes

VOLCANOES have played a part in forming some very hard and expensive minerals. The best of these are used as **gemstones** in rings and other jewellery. Hard volcanic rocks are also used for building. Mining is a common sight in areas where there are volcanoes that are active, dormant or extinct.

Diamonds are forever

Diamonds are the hardest and most expensive of all the gemstones. Diamonds are a form of **carbon**. Carbon is common in nature but it takes very special conditions to turn it into a diamond. The carbon has to be baked at great temperatures and compressed under great pressure for a diamond to be formed. These are the kind of conditions found in the narrow pipes that lead from magma chambers to volcanoes. One theory among geologists is that diamonds are formed in these volcanic pipes.

Some diamonds are found still in their original volcanic pipes. They are also found in sands and gravel which have been washed downstream by rivers. These have come from volcanic pipes that have been worn away by the weather. Diamonds are so hard that even the river cannot break them up. Diamonds are used for cutting into other rocks. The drills used to explore for oil have hard diamond teeth.

Useful rocks and minerals

Another useful mineral found in volcanic areas is **sulphur**. This is a yellow coloured mineral that gives Yellowstone National Park in the USA its name. Much of the sulphur comes up with hot water from underground. It stains the rock yellow, but can also build up thick layers that can be mined. Another name for sulphur is **brimstone**. Fire and brimstone are mentioned in Bible stories as the cause of death and destruction. Sulphur has many different uses. Sulphuric acid is often used in experiments in science laboratories.

Photo notes
- Diamonds are mined in Africa.
- Diamonds formed from carbon by great heat and pressure near a volcano.
- Diamonds are sometimes found in sands and gravel washed downstream in rivers.

Rocks can be changed by the great heat and pressure from volcanoes and their magma reservoirs. This is one way that metamorphic rocks are formed. **Marble** is an example of this. It is formed when **limestone** is baked and compressed.

Metals such as **tin** and **copper** are also formed by this kind of baking. Heat melts the metal minerals until they run through the surrounding rock in thin **veins**. These are also called **lodes**.

Volcanic rocks such as granite and basalt are not valuable, but they are very hard and have some uses. They both make strong building stone. Their shiny surfaces can look very attractive when polished.

China clay is a soft white substance that comes from granite. Steam from hot underground water has passed through the granite and rotted the feldspar. The result is a soft clay called **kaolin**. High pressure hoses are used to wash the china clay away from the quartz and mica which make up the granite. The china clay is then used in making paper, paint and medicine,

as well as china cups and plates. It is also used in ceramics which are important to modern industries such as electronics.

Pumice stone from volcanic eruptions is used as a rubbing stone. It is very light because of the holes left by bubbles of gas, but it is also very hard. Rafts of pumice can be left floating on the sea after a volcanic eruption.

Photo notes
- A china clay quarry in Cornwall.
- China clay has been formed from feldspar in granite.
- The cottage has been built using granite which is plentiful in the area.

Volcanoes and tourists

VOLCANOES make interesting tourist attractions. There is something about their power that makes people look at them with respect. Perhaps the idea of danger also adds to the enjoyment.

Visiting volcanoes

Some volcanoes are visited by thousands of people every year. The volcanic island of Lanzarote is one of the most popular of the Canary Islands. The Timanfaya volcano at the centre of the island is a popular tourist attraction. The area around the volcano has been made into a National Park that people can visit and enjoy. One restaurant in the National Park cooks its food over an open pit using heat from the volcano's hot rocks. On Lanzarote the sand is black because it has come from the black basalt and other volcanic rocks that have made the island.

In the USA, several of the National Parks take their names from the volcanoes that are in them. The Lassen and Rainier National Parks are two examples. Both Lassen and Rainier are active volcanoes with a history of violent eruptions. These areas are also the home of many species of plants and wildlife.

In New Zealand, the steep slopes of volcanoes in the Mount Cook and Mount Tasman National Parks are used for skiing and mountain climbing.

Photo notes

- Tourists on Volcano Island near Sicily.
- The yellow colour is sulphur which comes to the surface of the volcano through holes called fumaroles.

DID YOU KNOW?

In Hawaii, the volcanoes are visited by tourists who want to see a volcano erupting. The eruptions are not usually violent though they can produce a large amount of fast-flowing lava. In 1990, a lava flow destroyed the visitor centre.

Curious people

Other volcanic features are smaller and less spectacular but are still popular with visitors. Geysers, mudpots and fumaroles all attract people's interest. In New Zealand, people visit the springs and geysers at Rotorua. In Iceland, the Stokkur geyser can be relied on to erupt every three minutes. In the USA, the Yellowstone and Lassen National Parks also have these volcanic features.

The Roman town of Pompeii is a different kind of tourist attraction caused by a volcano. When Vesuvius erupted in AD79, the town was covered in ash that killed most of the 2000 people who lived there. The town and everything in it were preserved as a perfect fossil of its time. Casts have been made of the bodies of people who were trying to escape. Almost every detail from the day of the eruption has been captured.

In France, visitors come to the Volcanoes National Park in the Massif Central. There are no active volcanoes here any more. Instead, there are the remains of old cones and **puys**. The puys make good viewpoints from which to look over the rest of the landscape. Many of the old craters have lakes that are used for recreation.

One of the most unusual volcanoes to attract tourists is Mount Erebus in the Antarctic. A New Zealand airline flies tourists to see the volcano. The aircraft circles the volcano then flies back to New Zealand again. It is impossible to land anywhere near Mount Erebus.

Photo notes
- The Roman town of Pompeii is a popular tourist spot.
- Vesuvius volcano is in the background.
- Pompeii was destroyed when Vesuvius erupted in AD79.
- Volcanic ash has preserved the town.

Blown apart

Photo notes
- St Helens after the 1980 eruption.
- A gaping hole has been blown through the wall of the crater.
- New lava has started to build up another cone inside the crater.
- This volcano is still active but there is no way of knowing when it will erupt again.

THE shape of volcanoes can change very quickly. One giant eruption can blow away the top of the cone or a large part of its side. This does not happen very often but, when it does, the effects on both people and the landscape can be dramatic.

Changing shape

The Mount St Helens eruption of 1980 was one of the most violent eruptions in recent times. Before the eruption, the shape of the 2870 metre volcano was an almost perfect cone. Snow and ice covered the crater. The force of the eruption blew out one side of the crater and also part of the top. The volcano is now 400 metres lower and there is a clear view into the crater. The shape of the surrounding landscape has also changed. Mudflows and rock debris have filled the river valleys and lakes and a new layer of ash lies on the ground.

The volcano is still changing its shape. Inside the crater, a new vent has opened up and lava has started to build up a new cone. On the outside, rain and ice are starting to wear away the slopes and carve new valleys in the surrounding land. The life story of this volcano is very far from being over.

Collapsed cones

Some eruptions are so violent that a large part of the cone is blown away and the crater walls collapse. Only a low wide circular shape is left where the cone used to be. The remaining part of the crater is called a **caldera**.

The largest caldera on Earth is in the eastern part of the Mediterranean Sea where the Thera volcano used to be. Only the scattered Santorini islands are left to show what used to be there.

A caldera is usually formed where there is a large reservoir of magma close to the surface. An eruption empties the crater of its lava, leaving a hollow. The force of the explosion and the weight of the remaining part of the cone cause the walls of the crater to collapse.

Crater Lake in Oregon is all that is left of a volcano named Mount Mazama. This volcano erupted violently about 6600 years ago. A smaller volcano grew in the lake but this is now extinct. It forms an island called Wizard Island.

The most recent explosion on this scale was when Krakatoa erupted in 1883.

A large part of the cone was blasted away. The rest collapsed into the empty crater.

Calderas seem to form when a volcano is reaching the end of its active life. It is certainly a spectacular and very dangerous way to go. At least 36 000 people died when Krakatoa erupted. Most of the deaths were caused by the giant waves that washed over the low islands for hundreds of kilometres around the volcano. There is very little that would stop the same kind of disaster happening again.

DID YOU KNOW?

The noise from the explosion at Krakatoa was heard 4700 km away in Australia. No volcano has caused so many deaths since this eruption in 1883.

Extinct volcanoes

THERE are many places where the remains of old volcanoes can be seen. The volcanoes erupted far back in **geological time**, tens and even hundreds of millions of years ago. They are usually far from the edge of the present plates but they show where plates have been in the past. Lava and other igneous rocks are usually much harder than sedimentary rocks so they take longer to be worn away. This means that the rocks from volcanoes are left standing out as higher ground.

Old cones

There are many cones of extinct volcanoes in France, mostly in the Auvergne district of the Massif Central. Volcanoes were active there about 30 million years ago, when the Alps were being folded up and the ground was being cracked.

There are also narrow steep-sided features that point up like fingers. These are called puys. The Puy de Sancy and the Puy de Dome are two of the highest and most well known. They show where sticky magma came up into a volcano's vent, then cooled to become solid rock. The rest of the volcano has been worn away and only the hard magma is left.

The city of Edinburgh is built on the site of a volcano that erupted 300 million years ago. The city and its castle were build on top of steep volcanic crags. This made the site difficult to attack.

The last remains

Ship Rock stands alone in the New Mexico desert. It is all that is left of an old volcano. This is called a volcanic plug.

> **Photo notes**
> - Several old volcanic cones in the Auvergne district of France.
> - The cones are still rounded but their tops have been worn down and have collapsed into their craters.
> - There are lakes in some of the craters.

When the volcano stopped erupting, magma inside it cooled down inside and on top of the vent and became hard rock. All the softer rock that made the slopes of the volcano have been worn down around it. The whole landscape has been worn down leaving Ship Rock still standing. The remains of an old dike are nearby. This stands out as a steep ridge. The dike was probably a flow of lava that forced its way from the old volcano through layers of rock around it. Now all the older, softer rock has been worn away. The plug and the dike are both being worn away by weathering but the softer rock around them will always be worn away faster.

Sometimes, igneous rocks from magma chambers that were deep beneath old volcanoes are exposed after millions of years. The rock in these chambers has cooled slowly, forming granite which is very hard. Upland areas such as Dartmoor show where huge areas of magma cooled. These areas are old **batholiths**.

Pieces of broken rock are carried away by rivers, wind and sometimes by moving ice. If they reach the sea, they are washed along the coast by waves and currents. Some of the best sandy beaches are in areas where there is granite. This is because the sand is mostly tiny fragments of quartz and mica, two of the minerals in granite.

In time, the broken pieces of rock will be covered and compressed by other pieces. This makes layers of new sedimentary rocks such as **sandstone**. These new rocks may be carried along on a plate and be melted in a subduction zone. Then a **rock cycle** will have been completed as the same pieces are used to make new rock.

DID YOU KNOW?

Hadrian's Wall was built to protect Roman Britain from Picts in Scotland. A large part of the wall was built on a ridge with a steep side that faces Scotland. The ridge is the remains of a sill that forced its way through the surrounding rocks about 300 million years ago. The igneous rock that makes the sill has lasted very well.

Volcanoes and the weather

THE most powerful volcanic eruptions blast rock, soil, lava and gases high into the atmosphere. Any changes to the atmosphere can affect the weather. Historic records and satellite information show that some volcanic eruptions can affect weather patterns around the world.

Dust clouds

The force of a volcanic explosion shatters the material into tiny pieces of ash and dust. Heavier material falls back to the ground near the volcano. Lighter pieces are carried hundreds of kilometres before they fall either on their own or in rain.

The lightest pieces of dust are kept in the air by strong winds which circle the Earth carrying the dust with them. An effect of this is red evening skies. The sinking sun reflects on the dust and the sky glows red.

Dust and other gases from an eruption are able to stay in the atmosphere for several months. Dust may be able to affect the weather by making it rain more often. Raindrops form around tiny pieces of dust that are usually in the atmosphere. This means that more rain can be expected after extra dust has been added by a volcano.

Lightning is sometimes seen in the cloud of dust and ash above a volcano. One idea is that particles of dust become charged with electricity, causing giant electrical sparks in the cloud. Whatever the cause, the results are very spectacular.

Photo notes
- A cloud of dust and ash erupts from the Sakura-Jima volcano in Japan.
- Dust particles are charged with electricity which causes lightning in the clouds.

Long term changes

Some of the effects of an eruption may be felt for several years. These effects may be caused by both the dust and the gases.

More dust in the atmosphere should mean that less heat from the sun gets through to the ground. After the Tambora and Krakatoa eruptions in 1815 and 1883, less sunlight gave some very cold winters in some parts of the world. Dust from the eruptions may have been the cause of this.

The lack of sunlight is made worse by the fact that cold air sinks. The weight of sinking air causes high pressure on the ground. This is called an **anticyclone**. In winter, cold sinking air can give long periods of very cold weather.

Temperature affects the amount of water held in the air as **water vapour**. Air at higher temperatures hold more water vapour than colder air. If the temperature falls, the water vapour **condenses** to form rain. If it is cold enough, snow falls.

More heat is reflected back to space from white ground than from darker coloured ground. This would make it even colder so more snow would fall. At worst, the lower temperatures caused by erupting volcanoes could trigger another Ice Age.

In 1991, a satellite watched the dust cloud from the Mount Pinatubo eruption as it went around the Earth. It recorded the amount of sulphur dioxide gas that the volcano had ejected. Sulphur dioxide mixes with rainwater and forms **acid rain**. Acid rain damages or kills trees, plants, and the wildlife that depends on them.

Another gas from volcanic eruptions is carbon dioxide. This gas allows heat to come through the atmosphere but it stops it going out again. This is why it is called a **greenhouse gas**.

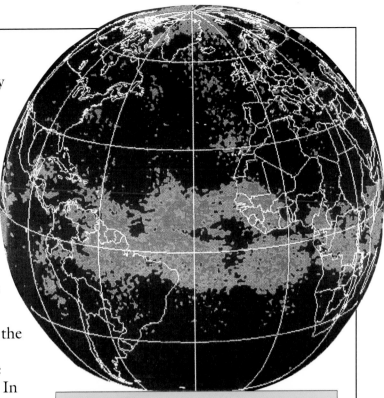

Photo notes
- This image was taken eighteen days after the Mount Pinatubo eruption.
- The green colour shows where there was most sulphur dioxide.
- The gas and dust cloud had moved half-way around the world and to the Atlantic Ocean.

People are already worried that more carbon dioxide from burning coal, wood and oil may be increasing the temperature of the Earth. More carbon dioxide from volcanoes would add to amounts that are already too high.

DID YOU KNOW?

The amount of dust, ash and other material that erupts from volcanoes varies greatly. The amount from some major eruptions is shown below.

Volcano name	Date of eruption	Cubic km
Mount Mazama	4600 BC	20
Vesuvius	AD 79	3
Tambora	AD 1815	50
Katmai	AD 1912	10
Mount St Helens	AD 1980	0.25

Volcanoes on Mars

EARTH is not the only planet where there are volcanoes. The highest and the widest known volcano is on Mars. This has been photographed by satellites that have flown past the planet. Finding out about volcanoes on Earth can help us understand more about Mars and the other planets. Studying the volcanoes on Mars and other planets may also help us understand more about the volcanoes on Earth.

The Olympus Mons

Olympus Mons is the name that has been given to the largest volcano on Mars. It is 26.4 km high and 600 km across its base. It looks like a very large shield volcano so it may have been formed in the same way as the volcanoes in Hawaii. There are no signs that Olympus Mons or any other volcano on Mars is still active. It would be interesting to find out when and why they stopped erupting.

The volcano is unusual because it is so large. This may mean that it erupted many times over a much longer time than the volcanoes on Earth. There may be other explanations you can think of.

Olympus Mons is in an area of Mars called the Tharsis bulge. This is an area where the surface has bulged out. Perhaps the bulge has made the planet's surface crack. This would allow magma to escape so that volcanoes could form. Several other volcanoes are nearby and the whole area looks as if it has been formed by lava flows. These may be flood basalts like those on the Earth. It could be useful to find out why the bulge was formed and if the same thing could happen on Earth.

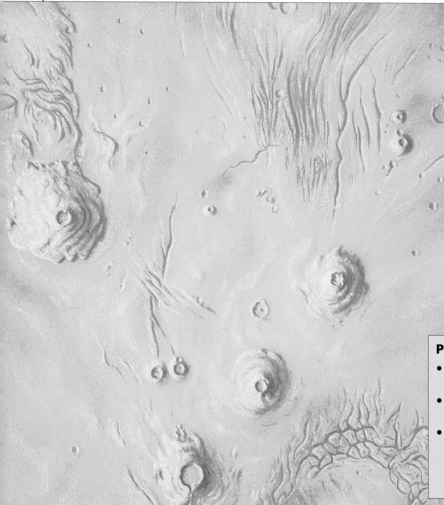

Photo notes
- Olympus Mons is shown in the top left of the photograph.
- Several more smaller volcanoes can also be seen.
- Curving lines on the photograph may be deep ravines caused by cracks in Mars' crust.

Inside the red planet

The volcanoes give some clues about what is inside Mars. At one time, there must have been molten material inside the planet. Some of this material must have escaped through volcanoes and fissures. Perhaps the volcanoes have stopped erupting because the inside of Mars has cooled down.

There are signs of cracks on the planet's surface. These may be like the fault lines that run along the edge of plates on the Earth. This could mean there are plates that used to move on Mars. The volcanoes may be extinct because plates have stopped moving.

One spacecraft that landed on Mars did not record any earthquakes. This could mean that the plates are not moving or even that there are no plates.

The Tharsis bulge and the volcanoes that sit on it must be very heavy. This may mean that Mars has a very strong, thick crust. Some scientists think the crust must be about 200 km thick. Perhaps the crust was not always that thick and volcanoes erupted when the crust was thinner.

There are many other questions that can be asked about the volcanoes on Mars, the Earth and on other planets and moons. One day, a spacecraft may land on Olympus Mons and maybe someone will walk on it. Then some of the right questions may be asked about how volcanoes work and some of the right answers may be found.

DID YOU KNOW? ?

Some of the most active volcanoes in the Solar System are on a moon named Io. This is one of several moons that orbit the planet Jupiter. Ten volcanoes were erupting on Io when the Voyager spacecraft flew past it in 1979.

Glossary

aa pasty lava that cools to form blocks of rock

acid rain rainwater mixed with chemicals

active a volcano that still erupts regularly is active

anticyclone weather area where air pressure is high

ash very fine pieces of material blown out of a volcano

basalt type of igneous rock that often forms from lava

batholith mass of molten rock that collects in the bottom part of the crust

brimstone sulphur

caldera the hollow left after a volcano collapses

carbon a chemical element

cap cooled lava that blocks a volcano's crater

china clay feldspar that has been rotted from granite

cinder small piece of volcanic material thrown out during an eruption

composite cone volcanic cone made from layers of different materials

condense to change from a gas to a liquid

cone rounded and pointed shape of many volcanoes

conelet small cone on the side of a larger volcano (parasitic cone)

continental plates large pieces of the Earth's crust with a continent on them

convection currents movements caused by heating

copper a type of metal formed naturally in rock

crater the wide opening at the top of a volcano

crust the upper hard layer of the Earth

crystal small part of a mineral

dense close together

dike flow of lava that passes through layers of rock

dormant a volcano that has not erupted for many years

dust the smallest material blasted out during a volcanic eruption

effusive a type of volcanic eruption when lava flows out over the crater rim

energy power

eruption the explosion caused by a volcano

extinct a volcano that will never erupt again is extinct

extrusive rock igneous rock that comes to the surface

feldspar a mineral found in rocks such as granite

fertile good for growing crops

fissure crack

flood basalt a massive flow of lava from a crack

fumarole small opening which emits steam and gasses

gas material in a state that is neither solid or liquid

gemstone a hard mineral often used for jewellery

geological era a division of geological time

geological time periods of time measured in millions of years

geologist a person who studies rocks

geothermal energy energy from hot rock beneath the Earth's surface

geyser a regular spurt of steam and hot water from under the ground

greenhouse gas a gas that absorbs heat

hot spot place where magma currents rise under the crust

hot spring hot water flowing from underground

hydrothermal water heated by hot rocks

igneous rock a group of rocks that come from under the crust

inner core the central part of the Earth

intrusive rock igneous rock that does not reach the surface

island arcs groups of island volcanoes in a curved line

kaolin feldspar that has been rotted from granite

land mass a very large area of land such as a continent

landslide rocks and soil that collapse down a slope

lava molten rock that flows from a volcano or a fissure

lava tube a hollow 'cave' left when lava drains away leaving a hard outer shell

laser a type of light (Light Amplification by Stimulated Emission of Radiation)

limestone a type of sedimentary rock formed under a sea

lode a thin deposit of a metal through a rock (vein)

lower mantle the layer inside the Earth between the upper mantle and the outer core

magma melted rock under the Earth's surface

magma chamber a reservoir of magma beneath a volcano

mantle layer inside the Earth between the crust and the core

marble a metamorphic rock formed when limestone is heated and compressed

mica mineral that forms part of other rocks such as granite

mineral a pure substance that combines with other minerals to form rocks

molten rock that is heated until it melts is molten

mudflow soil and mud that slides down a slope

mudpot a small mound of mud formed around an eruption of hot water

mud volcano large mound of mud formed around an eruption of hot water

nuée ardente hot and glowing cloud of volcanic material

observatory a building from which to watch and study

obsidian a black and glassy type of igneous rock

oceanic plate piece of Earth's crust with an ocean on it

outer core the layer inside the Earth between the inner core and the lower mantle

Pacific Ring of Fire the name given to the line of volcanoes around the Pacific Ocean

pahoehoe fluid lava that cools to look like piles of rope

parasitic cone a small cone on the side of a volcano (conelet)

pillow lava round shaped lava formed on the sea bed

pipe narrow tube between a magma reservoir and a volcano

plateau a flat topped upland with steep sides

plates separate parts of the Earth's crust

plate tectonics the movement of the Earth's plates

Plinian explosion a type of violent volcanic eruption

plug lava that cools in a volcano's vent

porous a rock that water can sink through is porous

power station a building where electricity is generated

prediction forecast

pumice a volcanic rock with holes from gas bubbles

puy a spine of volcanic rock that hardened in the vent and was exposed when the volcano eroded

quartz a mineral found in many types of rock

rim edge of a volcano's crater

rock cycle the way rocks form, break down and then reform

sandstone a type of sedimentary rock

satellite image a picture processed from electronic data received from a satellite

sedimentary rock a group of rocks formed from small pieces

seismometer instrument to measure ground movements

shield volcano volcano with shallow angled slopes

silica common mineral found in many types of rock

sill a layer of volcanic rock that has been squeezed between other layers of rock

steam eruption a volcanic eruption with large amounts of boiled water

subduction zone area where one plate slides beneath another

sulphur a type of mineral often found in volcanic areas

superheated heated to beyond boiling point, but prevented from boiling by being under high pressure

theory idea that seems right

tiltmeter an instrument to measure if slopes are changing their angle

tin a type of metal

tuff ash mixed with large pieces of volcanic material

trench very deep part of the ocean bed where one plate slides beneath another

turbine blades or a wheel, spun around by gas or liquid

typhoon hurricane

upper mantle the layer inside the earth between the crust and the lower mantle

vein a thin deposit of a metal through a rock (lode)

vent the place where lava comes out of a volcanic pipe

viscous thick and sticky

volcanic bomb lump of volcanic rock, rounded as it is thrown through the air

water vapour water in the form of a gas

weathering ways in which the weather breaks down rock

Index

Volcanoes in this book are shown in bold.